A Benjamin Blog and His Inquisitive Dog Guide

Mexico

Anita Ganeri

Heinemann
LIBRARY

Chicago, Illinois

© 2015 Heinemann Library
an imprint of Capstone Global Library, LLC
Chicago, Illinois

Edited by Dan Nunn, Helen Cox Cannons, and Gina Kammer
Designed by Jo Hinton-Malivoire
Picture research by Ruth Blair and Hannah Taylor
Production by Helen McCreath
Originated by Capstone Global Library Ltd
Printed and bound in China by Leo Paper Group

18 17 16 15 14
10 9 8 7 6 5 4 3 2 1

Library of Congress
Cataloging-in-Publication Data
Cataloging-in-publication information is on file with the Library of Congress.
ISBN 978-1-4109-6664-3 (hardcover)
ISBN 978-1-4109-6673-5 (paperback)
ISBN 978-1-4109-6691-9 (eBook PDF)

Acknowledgments
We would like to thank the following for permission to reproduce photographs:

Alamy: aerialarchives.com, 8, All Canada Photos, 11, Charles O. Cecil, 21, EPA European Pressphoto Agency B.V., 22, Eye Ubiquitous, 20, Martin Norris Travel Photography, 26, 29, North Wind Picture Archives, 7, Rafael Ben-Ari, 6, Ricky Schneider, 25; Corbis: Robert van der Hilst, 14; Getty Images: DEA/G. Dagli Orti, 12, Gamma-Rapho, 19, Minden Pictures/Tui De Roy, 10, Steven House Photography/House Light Gallery, 27, Travel Ink, 13; Shutterstock: Elena Elisseeva, 4, Globe Turner, 28, holbox, cover, RIRF Stock, 9; Superstock: age fotostock, 24, age fotostock/Jim West, 16, age fotostock/Judy Bellah, 18, Melvyn Longhurst, 15, Robert Harding Picture Library, 23, Universal Images Group, 17

007017LEOF14

Some words are shown in bold, **like this**. You can find out what they mean by looking in the glossary.

Contents

Welcome to Mexico!

Hello! My name is Benjamin Blog and this is Barko Polo, my **inquisitive** dog. (He is named after ancient ace explorer, **Marco Polo**.) We have just gotten back from our latest adventure—exploring Mexico. We put this book together from some of the blog posts we wrote on the way.

Mexico
Topographical Map

Mexicali

Ciudad Juárez

UNITED STATES

UNITED STATES

Sierra Madre Occidental

Conchos River

Yaqui River

Fuerte R.

Río Bravo del Norte

Río Grande

Sierra Madre Oriental

Bolsón de Mapimí

Torreón

Monterrey

Bala California

Gulf of California

PACIFIC OCEAN

Central Plateau

Gulf of Mexico

Islas Marías

Río Grande de Santiago

León

Pónuco R.

Cancún

Yucatán Peninsula

Isla Cozumel

Islas Revillagigedo

Guadalajara

Valley of Anáhuac

Popocatépetl

Veracruz

Mexico City

Pico de Orizaba

Usumacinta River

BELIZE

Bolsas River

Grijalva River

GUATEMALA

Sierra Madre del Sur

Oaxaca

Isthmus of Tehuantepec

Acapulco

Gulf of Tehuantepec

N
W   E
S

0   100   200 mi.
0 100 200 km

BARKO'S BLOG-TASTIC MEXICO FACTS
Mexico is a country in the southern part of North America. On one side is the Pacific Ocean and on the other, the Gulf of Mexico. On land, Mexico is joined to the United States, Belize, and Guatemala.

Story of Mexico

Posted by: Ben Blog | June 1 at noon

We arrived in Mexico City, and I headed straight for the museum to see the Sun Stone—an ancient Aztec calendar. The Aztecs ruled a great **empire** in Mexico from around 1300 to 1521. They were famous for being fierce warriors and for worshipping many gods and goddesses.

BARKO'S BLOG-TASTIC MEXICO FACTS

In 1519, the Spanish arrived in Mexico. They destroyed the Aztec Empire and stole its gold. This image shows a meeting between Hernán Cortés, the Spanish leader, and the Aztec **emperor** Montezuma.

Volcanoes, Rivers, and Deserts

Posted by: Ben Blog | June 15 at 8:46 a.m.

From Mexico City, we took the bus to Mexico's most famous mountain—Popocatépetl. You can see it from the city, but it is even more spectacular close up. It is an active volcano, which last erupted in 2013 and could blow its top at any time.

BARKO'S BLOG-TASTIC MEXICO FACTS

The longest river in Mexico is the Rio Grande. Its name means "Big River." It flows for around 1,900 miles (3,060 kilometers) from Colorado, in the U.S., to the Gulf of Mexico.

I snapped this gray whale and her baby in Baja California. Each year, hundreds of gray whales arrive here. They swim more than 6,214 miles (10,000 kilometers) from the Arctic Ocean to have their babies in the **lagoons**.

BARKO'S BLOG-TASTIC MEXICO FACTS

This is a lizard called a Gila (say "heela") monster. It lives in the desert in Mexico. In the daytime, it gets baking hot in the desert. Gila monsters stay cool in their underground burrows, then come out at night to hunt for food.

City Sightseeing

Posted by: Ben Blog | August 26 at 9:55 a.m.

Mexico City is the capital of Mexico. It is built on top of the ancient Aztec city of Tenochtitlán. I am here in the Zocalo, a huge square in the center of the city. This is where the Aztecs had their main temple—you can still see the ruins.

BARKO'S BLOG-TASTIC MEXICO FACTS

Many people go to the city of Acapulco for a vacation. I am here to see the famous cliff divers. They dive 148 feet (45 meters) off a clifftop into a narrow stretch of sea. Rather them than me!

Buenos Días

Posted by: Ben Blog | September 20 at 4:59 p.m.

Most people in Mexico have Spanish and Indian **ancestors**. They are called mestizos. The people in this photo are Nahua Indians, and they have Aztec ancestors. They have kept their languages and customs, and often wear traditional clothes.

Zócalo - Catedral →

Templo de la Compañía →

Palacio de Gobierno →

These Mexican children begin their school day by singing the **national anthem**. They start school at the age of 6 and learn Spanish, history, math, English, and other subjects. Some poorer children leave school before they are 16 to work.

BARKO'S BLOG-TASTIC MEXICO FACTS

Many Mexicans are very poor. They look for work in the cities and live in crowded **shanty towns**. A few wealthy people own a lot of land and live on huge **estates** in the countryside, called haciendas.

Next, we traveled south to Oaxaca for the Day of the Dead festival. It was wonderful! It is the day when Mexicans remember loved ones who have died, but it is not at all gloomy. People take flowers to their loved ones' graves and set up **shrines** at home. Children dress up in skeleton costumes and buy spooky sugar skulls.

BARKO'S BLOG-TASTIC MEXICO FACTS

Most people in Mexico are **Roman Catholics**. On December 12, they celebrate Guadalupe Day. It is the feast day of Our Lady of Guadalupe, the **patron saint** of Mexico.

Tasty Tortillas

Posted by: Ben Blog | November 1 at 6:35 p.m.

It has been a long day, so we grabbed a bite to eat from one of the taco stands in the street. Tacos are tortillas (thin flatbreads) filled with meat, fish, beans, and cheese. We washed them down with a glass of agua fresca, which is fruit juice mixed with water and sugar.

BARKO'S BLOG-TASTIC MEXICO FACTS

Corn, beans, tomatoes, avocados, and chili peppers are all popular things to eat in Mexico. On special occasions, you might have turkey with mole, a tangy chili-and-chocolate sauce.

Soccer and Song

Posted by: Ben Blog | November 15 at 3:00 p.m.

Our next stop was Guadalajara, Mexico's second-biggest city. We are here to watch a soccer match between Mexico and Argentina. They have hundreds of thousands of fans. They are also fierce rivals.

BARKO'S BLOG-TASTIC MEXICO FACTS

You see mariachi bands like this one in streets and restaurants. The musicians play guitars, trumpets, and violins, and wear silver-studded cowboy outfits.

From Coffee to Oil Wells

Posted by: Ben Blog | November 30 at 9:19 a.m.

From Guadalajara, we headed south again to the state of Chiapas, which is famous for its coffee. We visited a **plantation** on the slopes of a volcano to see how the coffee beans grow. Sugar, cotton, and tobacco are also grown in Mexico and sold to other countries.

BARKO'S BLOG-TASTIC MEXICO FACTS
Oil is Mexico's most valuable **natural resource**.
This oil rig is in the Gulf of Mexico. It produces
nearly 3 million barrels of oil a day. That's an
awful lot of oil!

And Finally ...

The last stop on our tour was the amazing ancient city of Chichen Itza. It was built by the Maya people around 1,000 years ago. This is a photo I took of El Castillo (The Castle), a pyramid-shaped temple. It has 365 steps to the top, one for each day of the year.

BARKO'S BLOG-TASTIC MEXICO FACTS

This is Copper Canyon in the Sierra Madre mountains. It's actually a group of seven canyons more than 0.6 miles (1 kilometer) deep. A canyon is a deep, narrow valley made by a river running through it.

Mexico Fact File

Area: 758,449 square miles
(1,964,374 square kilometers)

Population: 116,220,000 (2013)

Capital city: Mexico City

Other main cities: Guadalajara; Monterrey

Language: Spanish

Main religion: Christianity (Roman Catholic)

Highest mountain: Pico de Orizaba
(18,700 feet/5,700 meters)

Longest river: Rio Grande (Rio Bravo del Norte)
(1,895 miles/3,050 kilometers)

Currency: Peso

Mexico Quiz

Find out how much you know about Mexico with our quick quiz.

1. What language is spoken in Mexico?
a) French
b) Spanish
c) German

2. What is a taco?
a) a drink
b) something to eat
c) a Mexican hat

3. What is a Gila monster?
a) a lizard
b) a fish
c) a bird

4. What do Mexican school children sing in the morning?
a) a nursery rhyme
b) a pop song
c) the **national anthem**

5. What is this?

Answers
1. b
2. b
3. a
4. c
5. El Castillo

Glossary

ancestor a relative from the past

emperor a person who rules a group of countries

empire a group of countries ruled by one country

estate a large piece of land in the countryside

inquisitive being interested in learning about the world

lagoon a body of water cut off from the sea

Marco Polo an explorer who lived from about 1254 to 1324; he traveled from Italy to China

national anthem a song that is special to a particular country

natural resource a natural material that we use, such as coal, oil, or wood

patron saint a holy person who is special to a particular country or person

plantation a large farm where crops, such as coffee or bananas, are grown

Roman Catholic a Christian who belongs to the Roman Catholic Church

shanty town a poor part of a town or city where people live in makeshift homes

shrine a holy place where people worship or place holy objects or images

Find Out More

Books

Alcraft, Rob. *A Visit to Mexico.*(A Visit To).
Chicago: Heinemann Library, 2008

Gagne, Tammy. *We Visit Mexico*
(Your Land and My Land).
Hockessin, Del.: Mitchell Lane, 2011

Savery, Annabel. *Mexico* (Been There).
Mankato, Minn.: Smart Apple Media, 2012

Websites

kids.nationalgeographic.com/kids/places
The National Geographic website has lots of
information, photos, and maps of countries around
the world.

www.worldatlas.com
Packed with information about various countries,
this website includes flags, time zones, facts, maps,
and timelines.

Index